CONTENTS

Rapper's Delight

In the summer of 1979, record producer Sylvia Robinson stopped in a pizza place. She listened to a young man rapping as he worked behind the counter. Robinson had heard a little bit about this new hip-hop scene. Impressed, Robinson signed the young man to a recording contract along with two of his friends.

The young man was Henry "Big Bank Hank" Jackson. He managed a hip-hop group from New York City. Jackson was joined by Guy "Master Gee" O'Brien and Michael "Wonder Mike" Wright. They called themselves the Sugarhill Gang.

The Sugarhill Gang was the first group Sylvia Robinson signed to her new label, Sugar Hill Records.

The Sugarhill Gang laid down a 15-minute rap over Chic's disco song "Good Times". They called their song "Rapper's Delight". Little did they know, the song they recorded would kick off a worldwide **phenomenon**.

Sugarhill Gang

Big Bank Hank

Wonder Mike

Master Gee

phenomenon ▸▸▸ *something very unusual or remarkable*

CHAPTER 1

Back in the day

When most people think about the beginnings of hip-hop, they remember "Rapper's Delight". They may also think about breakdancing, graffiti, DJ-ing, and MC-ing in the early 1980s. In reality, the origins of hip-hop reach back way before these artists ever started doing their thing.

Hip-hop is an American art form inspired by African-American music and culture. Starting in the 1950s, DJs in Jamaica played records at street parties. Before the first rap lyrics were ever spoken, jazz musicians would "scat sing" on their records. They used short syllables such as "be-bop" to create **rhythmic** sounds. Spoken-word poetry became popular in the 1960s. Jazz, blues, and soul artists of the 1950s, 1960s, and 1970s created tracks that would later be **sampled** in rap songs.

HIP-HOP INFLUENCES

Rap is influenced by a variety of music categories from North America, Jamaica, and Africa.

North America

DETROIT, PHILADELPHIA, & MEMPHIS:
Soul

NEW YORK:
Disco

WEST COAST:
Funk and Soul

MISSISSIPPI RIVER DELTA:
Blues

NEW ORLEANS:
Jazz

JAMAICA:
Reggae

Africa

WEST AFRICA:
Rhythmic lyrics, folk songs

rhythmic	*having a regular beat in music or dance*
sample	*to take a portion of one song and reuse it in another*

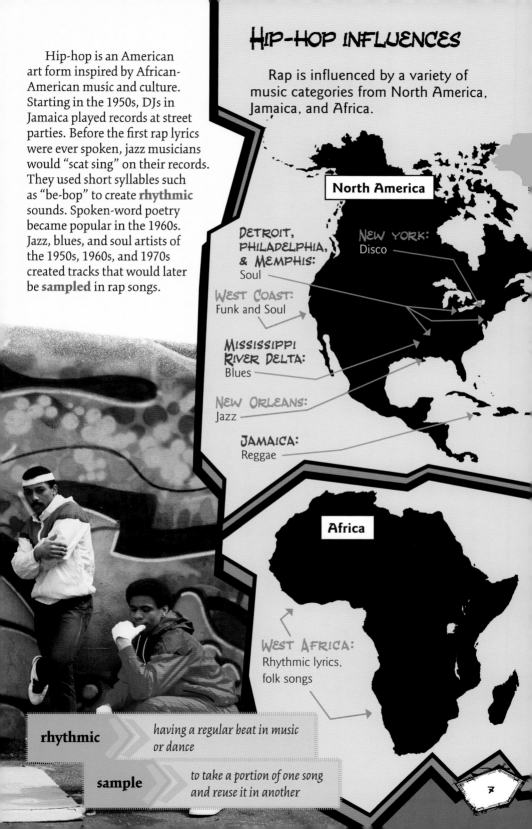

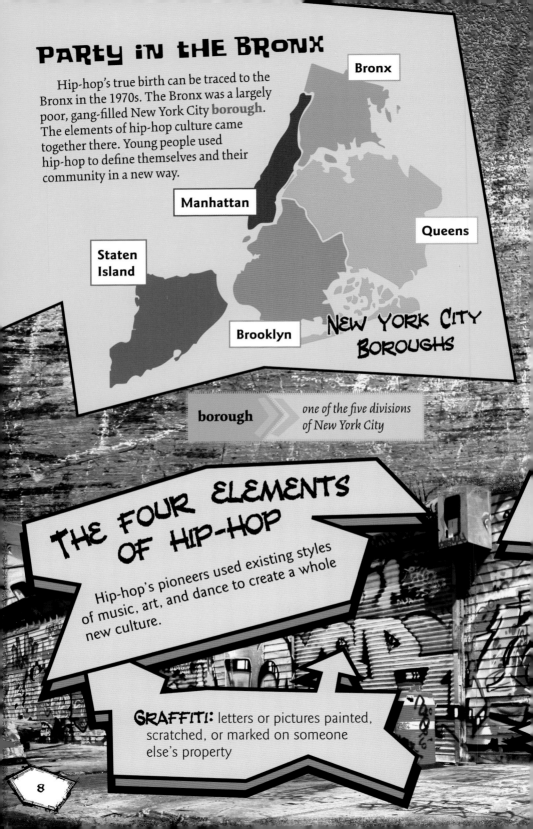

PARTY iN tHE BRONX

Hip-hop's true birth can be traced to the Bronx in the 1970s. The Bronx was a largely poor, gang-filled New York City **borough**. The elements of hip-hop culture came together there. Young people used hip-hop to define themselves and their community in a new way.

Bronx

Manhattan

Queens

Staten Island

Brooklyn

NEW YORK CITY BOROUGHS

borough ›› *one of the five divisions of New York City*

THE FOUR ELEMENTS OF HiP-HOP

Hip-hop's pioneers used existing styles of music, art, and dance to create a whole new culture.

GRAFFITI: letters or pictures painted, scratched, or marked on someone else's property

In the late 1960s, a young man in Philadelphia named Darryl "Cornbread" McCray started a new trend. He **tagged** his name in permanent marker on the walls of his school. Although this was an illegal activity, graffiti soon caught on with youths and gang members in New York City. Over time, graffiti developed to include spray paint, block letters, and images.

Then came the street parties, where DJ-ing, MC-ing, and breakdancing sprang up. And no one threw a street party like DJ Kool Herc.

Cornbread

tag	write one's name on public property in paint or permanent marker

DJ-ING: playing pre-recorded music for a radio, party, or club audience. *DJ* is short for *disc jockey*.

BREAKDANCING: a form of street dance that features footwork, floor work, and other acrobatic moves

MC-ING: rapping and rhyming over the beats of a DJ or producer. *MC* is short for *master of ceremonies*.

9

THE FATHER OF HIP-HOP

Clive "Kool Herc" Campbell is known as the father of hip-hop. Herc was born in Kingston, Jamaica. He grew up around Jamaica's powerful sound systems and street parties. Herc listened to James Brown and Motown records. In 1967, 12-year-old Herc moved to New York with his family, bringing his musical knowledge and tastes with him. He practised mixing records on his father's **turntables** in their Bronx apartment.

What's in a Name?

DJ Kool Herc was a strong and aggressive basketball player, which earned him the nickname "Hercules". He later shortened the name to "Herc".

Afrika Bambaataa

Kool Herc

| turntable | >> | circular, revolving surface used for playing phonograph records |

Herc DJ'd his first party in 1973. Instead of playing the whole song, he would set his records to the drum break. To make the break last longer, Herc bought two copies of the same record. Then he switched back and forth between them to feature the break section. This section became known as the "break beat". Dancers who got down to the break beats were called breakdancers, or b-boys and b-girls.

Kool Herc wasn't the only DJ throwing street parties in the Bronx. Former gang leader Kevin "Afrika Bambaataa" Donovan started DJ-ing as well. He formed a group with other DJs, breakdancers, MCs, and graffiti writers. Many were also former gang members. They worked hard to spread positive hip-hop culture. Bambaataa named his group the Zulu Nation. They breakdanced and wrote graffiti throughout the city. The Zulus even toured in Europe in the early 1980s, giving the continent its first taste of hip-hop.

ZULU NATION'S FOUNDATION

Afrika Bambaataa proved he was a leader for positive change. Even while a leader of the Black Spades gang, Bambaataa urged the Hispanic and black communities to join together. While still in high school in the early 1970s, he formed a group called the Organization. This group worked together to fight the threat of violence and drugs in the community. The Organization later became the foundation for the Zulu Nation.

MASTER OF CEREMONIES

Grandmaster Flash and the Furious Five

Grandmaster Flash

Barbados-born DJ Joseph "Grandmaster Flash" Saddler took hip-hop to a whole new level. MCs at Herc's and Bambaataa's parties called out simple phrases like "Clap ya hands to the beat, y'all". But Flash's MCs had an organized act. His five MCs, called the Furious Five, took turns rapping while Flash spun his records. They even came up with dance moves to go with their rhymes.

Flash and his crew developed a collection of popular DJ techniques still used today. In the mid-1970s, Flash's student DJ Theodore "Grand Wizard Theodore" Livingston invented the **needle drop** and the **scratch**. Flash perfected these techniques at his parties. He also introduced the beat box, a drum machine that he could play in time with a record.

Turn down that music!
Grand Wizard Theodore invented the scratch when his mother yelled at him to turn down his music. He held down a record with the needle still dropped.

needle drop	*action of dropping the needle on a specific spot on the record*
scratch	*action of moving a record back and forth while the needle is dropped*

By the late 1970s, MCs had a strong following in New York. They moved their parties from high school gyms and parks in the Bronx to dance clubs in Manhattan.

BE GOOD TO THE ROXY AND THE ROXY WILL BE GOOD TO YOU

To keep this night successful and ongoing, please be respectful to the club and the neighborhood.
Thank-you

Where are the girls at?

Sharon "Sha-Rock" Green was the first female MC to be part of a well-known crew. Her group, the Funky 4 + 1, became the first hip-hop crew to perform live on national TV. Sha-Rock was still a teenager when she appeared on *Saturday Night Live* in 1981.

Cold Crush Brothers

RAP'S FIRST HIT SONG

In a move that changed hip-hop history, Big Bank Hank borrowed a book of rhymes from the Cold Crush Brothers. He used some of their rhymes to get started on his own MC-ing career. The Cold Crush Brothers were a popular hip-hop group. One of their rhymes became the vocals for the hit "Rapper's Delight" by the Sugarhill Gang. The song reached number four on *Billboard's* R&B chart. But the Cold Crush Brothers never got credit. Nevertheless, rap had made it to the masses, and hip-hop would never be the same.

Popular Manhattan hip-hop clubs included the Ritz, Danceteria, and the Mudd Club. The Roxy was perhaps the most famous. Afrika Bambaataa and Grandmaster Flash often performed there in the early 1980s.

Taking over

The success of "Rapper's Delight" turned the spotlight from the DJ to the MC. Rap singles continued to create buzz heading into the 1980s.

Some of the first successful MCs were also b-boys. They made names for themselves at Bronx street parties and Manhattan disco clubs. One such b-boy was Kurtis Blow. He was the first rapper to be signed to a major record label, Mercury Records. In 1979, he recorded a funky version of the Christmas poem "The Night Before Christmas". The song "Christmas Rappin'" sold more than 600,000 copies worldwide.

Kurtis Blow was no one-hit wonder. He came back with the monster hit "The Breaks". This was the first rap single to be certified gold in the United States. It sold more than 1 million copies worldwide.

Kurtis Blow

The Recording Industry Association of America certifies a record as gold when it sells 500,000 copies.

RAPTURE

BLONDIE

PHOTOGRAPHER MARTIN HOFFMAN

Rap made its way into the pop band Blondie's 1981 smash "Rapture". Lead singer Debbie Harry rapped towards the end of the song. She even tipped her hat to hip-hop pioneers Grandmaster Flash and Fab 5 Freddy in the lyrics. The song was the first rap-influenced single to top the *Billboard* singles chart.

MAINSTREAM MOMENTUM

Inspired by the Sugarhill Gang and Kurtis Blow, more hip-hoppers cut records. Afrika Bambaataa and Grandmaster Flash released "Planet Rock" and "The Message" in the early 1980s. But a new hip-hop crew was about to take rap to a whole new level.

Three teenagers from Queens formed a rap group they called Run-DMC. They released the hit tracks "It's Like That" and "Sucker MCs" in 1983. Run-DMC had a sound like no other rap group. At the time, most rappers recorded their rhymes over disco and funk styles. But Run-DMC rapped over a drum machine and turntables. Hip-hop fans couldn't get enough of their new hard-hitting sound.

Run-DMC

In 1986, Run-DMC made history as the first MCs to appear on the cover of *Rolling Stone* magazine.

Run-DMC's most famous song is the 1986 remake of "Walk This Way" with rock band Aerosmith. The song cemented the relationship between rap and rock. It became the first rap single to reach the top 10 of *Billboard's* pop chart.

Beastie Boys

Rap trio the Beastie Boys also mixed rock with their raps. They started out as a punk rock band. In 1986, they released their first rap album, *Licensed to Ill*. A group of New York teens, the Beastie Boys used **rebellious** lyrics in their rhymes. They helped introduce rap to white audiences.

rebellious ⟫ disobedient to the people in charge

LL Cool J

Queens-born rapper LL Cool J was also gaining buzz in the mid-1980s. Def Jam Records signed him as its first artist in 1984. LL's smooth voice, baby face, and signature Kangol hat had a wide appeal. He won fans who hadn't paid much attention to rap music in the past.

LL Cool J was born James Todd Smith. His hip-hop name is short for "Ladies Love Cool James".

LL Cool J Albums

Radio (1985)

Bigger and Deffer (1987)

Walking with a Panther (1989)

Mama Said Knock You Out (1990)

14 Shots to the Dome (1993)

Mr. Smith (1995)

All World: Greatest Hits (1996)

Phenomenon (1997)

G.O.A.T. (2000)

10 (2002)

The DEFinition (2004)

Todd Smith (2006)

Exit 13 (2008)

LL's mainstream success angered some hip-hop pioneers. They thought he tried to sound too much like pop music. But LL kept the hits coming. He recorded rap ballads like "I Need Love" and tough-guy songs such as "Mama Said Knock You Out". Today, LL Cool J is a hip-hop **mogul**. He has found success as an actor, author, and fashion designer.

mogul ▷▷▷ *important or powerful person*

HiP-HoP GoES HollywooD

In the early 1980s, films about hip-hop began popping up. They brought hip-hop pioneers to the big screen and documented the beginning of a new culture.

Some films focused on **authentic** hip-hop culture:

- *Wild Style*, 1982. Director Charlie Ahearn cast real-life hip-hoppers to fill out his cast. Legendary graffiti writers Lee Quiñones and Sandra "Lady Pink" Fabara played lead roles in the film. Fab 5 Freddy, the Cold Crush Brothers, and Grandmaster Flash also appeared in the movie.

- *Style Wars*, 1983. Documentary filmmakers followed the lives of graffiti artists and breakdancers living in New York City. The film also featured citizens who disliked the graffiti that was taking over their city.

authentic >>> *real or genuine*

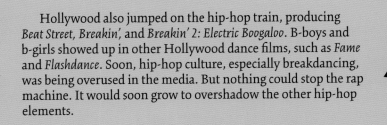

Hollywood also jumped on the hip-hop train, producing *Beat Street*, *Breakin'*, and *Breakin' 2: Electric Boogaloo*. B-boys and b-girls showed up in other Hollywood dance films, such as *Fame* and *Flashdance*. Soon, hip-hop culture, especially breakdancing, was being overused in the media. But nothing could stop the rap machine. It would soon grow to overshadow the other hip-hop elements.

The final scene from 1984's Breakin' 2: Electric Boogaloo *featured costumes and a detailed dance number.*

Did you know?
In her final dance scene in the film *Flashdance*, actress Jennifer Beals impresses judges with a fast-moving backspin. But Richard "Crazy Legs" Colon, Beals' stunt breaker, actually performed the move. He wore a wig and camouflaged his face.

THE SMALL SCREEN

In the 1980s, music videos were popular on MTV. But people didn't see much hip-hop until *Yo! MTV Raps* debuted in August 1988. The show was on the air for seven years, helping to introduce hip-hop culture to the world. Fred "Fab 5 Freddy" Braithwaite, James "Ed Lover" Roberts, and Andre "Doctor Dre" Brown hosted the show. *Yo!* featured both established and up-and-coming artists.

Ed Lover

Producer Ted Demme

Doctor Dre

Ed Lover created his own dance called "The Ed Lover Dance". Guests of the show had fun performing the hip-shaking dance.

FAMOUS FACES

Yo! MTV Raps hosted plenty of legendary MCs in its day. Here are some of the show's most memorable moments:

» In the first episode, female rap group Salt-N-Pepa invited Fab 5 Freddy to a music video rehearsal. Salt-N-Pepa also appeared on *Yo!'s* final episode.

» R&B singer Bobby Brown came on the show in 1989. His album *Don't Be Cruel* was the best-selling album of that year. Brown refused to appear on any other MTV show except *Yo! MTV Raps*.

» In 1990, Fab 5 Freddy met up with West Coast rappers and gang members in Los Angeles. They met to help promote peace in their neighbourhoods. Ice-T, N.W.A., and Digital Underground helped support the cause.

» In 1995, *Yo!* visited P. Diddy and the Notorious B.I.G. at the offices of up-and-coming rap label Bad Boy Records.

Hip-hop gets serious

Heading into the 1990s, three separate sounds developed in rap music. One was commercial rap, a style brought on by the success of MC Hammer and Vanilla Ice. With its playful beats and lyrics, commercial rap appealed to a wide audience.

MC Hammer

MC Hammer's 1990 album Please Hammer Don't Hurt 'Em *sold more than 10 million copies. It remains one of rap's best-selling albums.*

And then there was rap with a message. Rap group Public Enemy spoke out about social and political issues. Public Enemy front man Carlton "Chuck D" Ridenhour described this kind of hip-hop as "black America's CNN". Chuck D was considered the group's lead rapper. But William "Flavor Flav" Drayton gained fame for wearing an oversized clock that hung from a necklace. Flav's job was to get the crowd going. His clocks let everyone know it was time to get excited.

In 2004, Public Enemy was ranked number 44 on *Rolling Stone* magazine's list of Immortals: 100 Greatest Artists of All Time.

Public Enemy

Professor Griff

Terminator X

Chuck D

Flavor Flav

In the late 1980s, gang violence increased on the West Coast. Out of this uneasy environment, gangsta rap was born. Gangsta rap described the violence and difficulties of inner-city and gang life.

Gangsta rap's core MCs included Eric "Eazy-E" Wright, O'Shea "Ice Cube" Jackson, and Andre "Dr. Dre" Young. They formed a group called N.W.A. The group drew national attention for a song about dishonest police officers from their 1988 album *Straight Outta Compton*.

N.W.A. broke up in the early 1990s. Dr. Dre put out his first solo album, *The Chronic*, in 1992. Snoop Dogg, Dr. Dre's student, also rapped on the album. The pair became an unstoppable team of hit-makers with songs like "Nuthin' But a 'G' Thang" and "Let Me Ride".

Dr. Dre

N.W.A.

After N.W.A., Ice Cube went on to have a successful rapping and acting career. He has starred in *Boyz N the Hood*, *Barbershop*, and *The Longshots*.

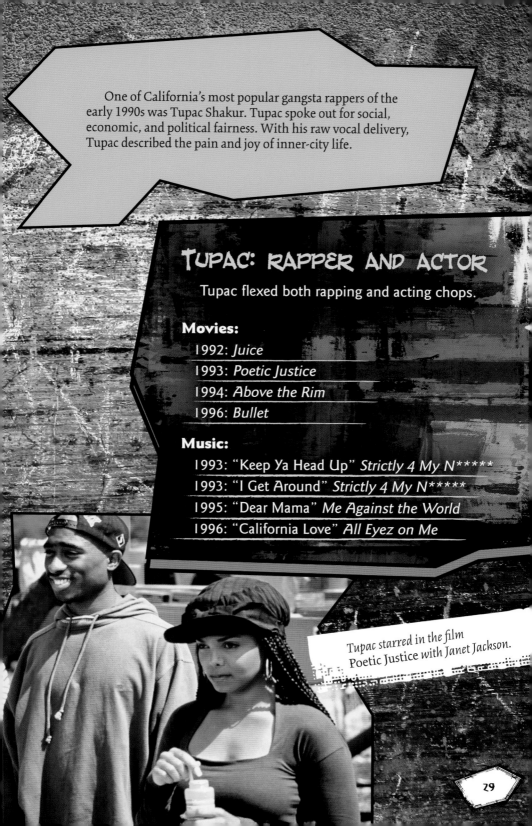

One of California's most popular gangsta rappers of the early 1990s was Tupac Shakur. Tupac spoke out for social, economic, and political fairness. With his raw vocal delivery, Tupac described the pain and joy of inner-city life.

TUPAC: RAPPER AND ACTOR

Tupac flexed both rapping and acting chops.

Movies:

1992:	*Juice*
1993:	*Poetic Justice*
1994:	*Above the Rim*
1996:	*Bullet*

Music:

1993:	"Keep Ya Head Up"	*Strictly 4 My N******
1993:	"I Get Around"	*Strictly 4 My N******
1995:	"Dear Mama"	*Me Against the World*
1996:	"California Love"	*All Eyez on Me*

Tupac starred in the film Poetic Justice with Janet Jackson.

EaSt coaSt v. WESt coaSt

The West Coast rappers seemed to have their fingers on the pulse of the hip-hop audience. By the mid-1990s, West Coast rappers outsold East Coast MCs.

The East Coast began to hit back with new rappers. Sean "P. Diddy" Combs found a star in Brooklyn rapper Christopher "Notorious B.I.G." Wallace, also called "Biggie Smalls". He signed Biggie, a talented writer, to his Bad Boy label. Biggie announced New York's comeback with hits such as "Big Poppa" and "One More Chance". New York rappers Shawn "Jay-Z" Carter, Busta Rhymes, and Nas also shifted the focus back East.

The Notorious B.I.G. originally recorded his demos under the name "Biggie Smalls". When he discovered Biggie Smalls was already in use by another rapper, he became the Notorious B.I.G.

This mural of the Notorious B.I.G. was painted in Queens, New York, in 2006.

The Source is a monthly magazine devoted to hip-hop, R&B, politics, and culture. The magazine hosted its first annual Source Awards in 1994 to recognize top hip-hop and R&B artists.

By 1995, there was a rivalry between the West Coast's Death Row Records and Bad Boy Records in the East. That year, Death Row president Suge Knight spoke out against P. Diddy at the Source Awards. Knight criticized P. Diddy for rapping on his artists' records and appearing in their music videos.

Tupac Shakur signed to Death Row Records in 1995. He recorded the song "Hit 'Em Up". In the song, Tupac slammed the Notorious B.I.G. and his crew. As bad feelings grew between the two groups, tragedy hit. In September 1996, Tupac was shot and killed in Las Vegas. In March 1997, the Notorious B.I.G. was murdered in Los Angeles. Neither of their murders was ever solved. Their deaths shook the hip-hop community.

BAD BOY V. DEATH ROW

Bad Boy Records
Founded in 1993 by P. Diddy
Notable Artists:

P. Diddy

Faith Evans

Mase

The Notorious B.I.G.

Total

Death Row Records
Founded in 1991 by Dr. Dre and Suge Knight
Notable Artists:

Dr. Dre

Bow Wow

Nate Dogg

Snoop Dogg

Tupac Shakur

MOVE OVER, BOYS

In the late 1980s, female rappers didn't match the success of male MCs. All that changed when Salt-N-Pepa released the album *Hot Cool & Vicious* in 1986.

At a time when gangsta rap ruled the charts, Salt-N-Pepa rocked fans with songs about love and having fun. They wrote tunes that celebrated women. Their biggest hit, the 1993 album *Very Necessary*, sold 5 million copies. In 1994, Salt-N-Pepa won the Grammy Award for Best Rap Performance by a Duo or Group. They proved that female rappers could be just as successful as their male counterparts.

Salt-N-Pepa

A Grammy is an award presented by the US Recording Academy to top recording artists. Each year, academy members vote for their favourites in styles such as rap, rock, pop, and country.

CHAPTER 4

Mo' Money, Mo' Problems

In the late 1990s, hip-hop would once again undergo a change. After the losses of Tupac Shakur and the Notorious B.I.G., the popularity of gangsta rap faded. The rap industry had become rich from nearly 20 years of best-selling album sales. Rap artists began to reflect this success in their songs.

Bad Boy Records was still reeling from the loss of its star. But other artists had hits of their own. P. Diddy came out from the sidelines with "I'll Be Missing You," a tribute to the Notorious B.I.G. He followed up with the hits "It's All About the Benjamins" and "Can't Nobody Hold Me Down". P. Diddy and his favourite sidekick Mase rapped the intro verses of Biggie's number-one hit "Mo' Money, Mo' Problems". They opened a flashy age of rapping about fashion labels, cars, and **bling**.

bling ›› *flashy jewellery sometimes worn to show wealth*

History of Bling

Rap artists B.G. and Cash Money Millionaires coined the word *bling* in the late 1990s. Cash Money artist Lil Wayne rapped about bling on his 1998 track "Millionaire Dream". B.G. named one of his songs on his 1999 album *Chopper City in the Ghetto* "Bling Bling". The song helped make the term even more popular. The phrase soon spread beyond hip-hop culture. It was added to the *Oxford Dictionary* in 2003 and to the US *Merriam-Webster* dictionary in 2006.

Lil' Kim

Female rappers Inga "Foxy Brown" Marchand and Kimberly "Lil' Kim" Jones also got in on the action. In their songs, they gave nods to their favourite designers – Prada, Versace, and Dolce & Gabbana.

HIP-HOP'S POWER PLAYERS

For years, companies have paid hip-hop stars to help sell their products. But some hip-hop artists and producers became moguls by starting their own companies.

P. Diddy heads up a hip-hop empire. He is the founder and CEO of Bad Boy Entertainment. His fashion label, Sean John, is a best-selling hip-hop line. P. Diddy is one of the wealthiest men in hip-hop today.

Jay-Z Carter joins P. Diddy in mogul status. He's the former President of Def Jam Records and has produced and rapped on best-selling albums. Jay-Z has invested in clothing lines, beverage companies, and clubs. He's even part owner of the New Jersey Nets basketball team.

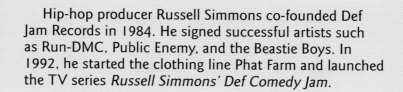

Hip-hop producer Russell Simmons co-founded Def Jam Records in 1984. He signed successful artists such as Run-DMC, Public Enemy, and the Beastie Boys. In 1992, he started the clothing line Phat Farm and launched the TV series *Russell Simmons' Def Comedy Jam*.

QuotE it

"It ain't about $200 sneakers. It is not about me being better than you or you being better than me. It's about you and me, connecting one on one. That's why it [hip-hop] has universal appeal. It has given young people a way to understand their world, whether they are from the suburbs or the city."

–DJ Kool Herc, from *Can't Stop Won't Stop* by Jeff Chang

THE NEW CLASS

In the 1980s and 1990s, most of hip-hop's popular rap artists came from New York or California. In the 2000s, Midwestern and Southern rappers got noticed for representing their hometowns.

Nelly

St Louis: In the early 2000s, Nelly put S. Louis, Missouri, on the map with his hits "Country Grammar" and "Hot in Herre". Rapper Chingy kept the Midwest going in 2003 with his debut hit "Right Thurr".

Minneapolis/St Paul: The Twin Cities has a rich underground hip-hop scene. Rap group Atmosphere has toured the world and sold more than 1 million albums. The group has earned praise from *Rolling Stone* and *Entertainment Weekly* magazines.

Ludacris

Atlanta: The South is a region that's now topping hip-hop record sales. Lil Jon, OutKast, and Ludacris introduced the region's bouncy, twangy flavour to rap. The style is often called crunk.

Kanye West

Chicago: Producer, rapper, and Chicago native Kanye West created a style all of his own. He is inspired by many types of music, including 1970s R&B, rock, and classical music. West's 2004 debut album, *The College Dropout*, earned 10 Grammy Award nominations.

Detroit: Eminem put out a string of hit records in the early 2000s. He has sold more than 27 million albums in the United States alone.

Minnesota

Minneapolis/ St Paul

Michigan

Detroit

Chicago

Illinois

Virginia

Portsmouth

St Louis

Missouri

Atlanta

Georgia

Portsmouth: After the success of her 1997 debut *Supa Dupa Fly*, Missy Elliott kept the hits coming in the 2000s. She is one of the top-selling female rappers.

Hip-hop is not limited to American shores. Pockets of hip-hop activity have sprung up in countries such as the United Kingdom, France, Germany, South Korea, and Japan. Europe and Asia are home to many graffiti artists. International b-boy festivals take place overseas. Rappers perform songs in many languages.

INTERNATIONAL HIP-HOP STARS

Many American MCs enjoy huge popularity overseas. But international hip-hop has its own stars as well.

France: MC Solaar
MC Solaar's 1991 album *Qui Sème le Vent Récolte le Tempo* put French rap music on the map.

Japan: Rhymester
This popular Japanese hip-hop group got its start in the late 1980s. They rap about political and social topics.

UK: Lady Sovereign
In 2005, Lady Sovereign became the first non-American female MC to sign with Def Jam Records.

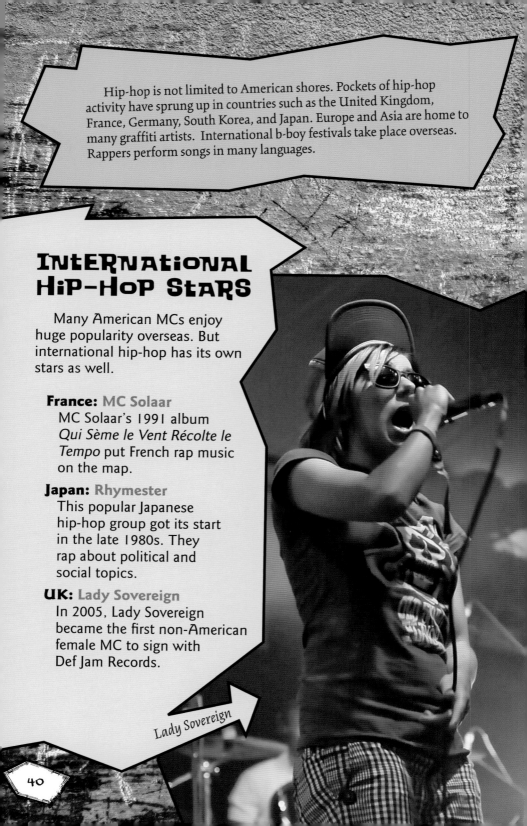

Lady Sovereign

BATTLE OF THE YEAR

Since 1990, b-boys and b-girls have battled it out in an annual event called Battle of the Year. Held in Germany, the international competition features breakdancing crews. Breakers face off in front of crowds of nearly 10,000. Crews are judged on stage presence, delivery, and the difficulty of their routines.

WHERE it's at

More than 30 years have passed since the release of hip-hop's first single. Young rap artists such as Lil Wayne, T-Pain, and T.I. continue to burn up the *Billboard* charts. Former **underground artists** Common, The Roots, and Mos Def also made their marks in recent years. They became known for socially-conscious songs. Common and Mos Def are now establishing themselves as Hollywood actors. They appeared in films such as *American Gangster* and *The Hitchhiker's Guide to the Galaxy*.

T-Pain

underground artist artist who is not signed to a major record label and is not considered part of the mainstream

Breakdancing and graffiti art have found new life. Hip-hop dance has its own TV show, *America's Best Dance Crew*. Several recent films, including *Step Up 2: The Streets* and *You Got Served*, featured breakdancing. Graffiti has been published in art books. Museums such as the Smithsonian and the Brooklyn Museum also display graffiti art.

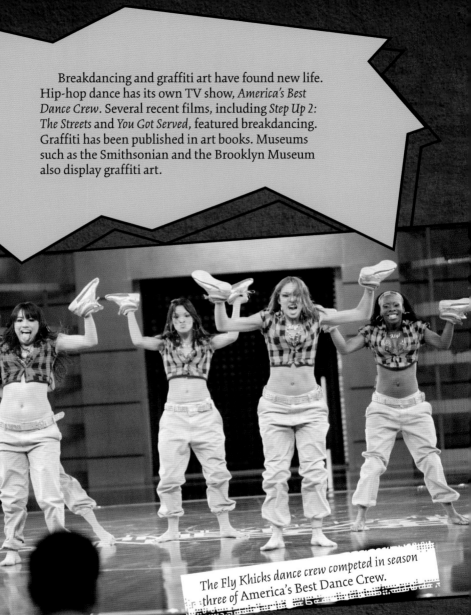

The Fly Khicks dance crew competed in season three of America's Best Dance Crew.

Hip-hop's story is far from over. What began on Bronx streets in the 1970s has become a way of life for many people. The worldwide popularity of DJ-ing, MC-ing, breakdancing, and graffiti is proof that hip-hop can't be stopped.

Hip-hop time line

Mid-1970s: Graffiti art spreads to cover New York City subway cars.

1986: Run-DMC pairs up with Aerosmith for the first rap and rock partnership on "Walk This Way".

1979: "Rapper's Delight" by the Sugarhill Gang hits airwaves.

1982: Afrika Bambaataa and the Soul Sonic Force release "Planet Rock".

1973: Kool Herc DJs his first street party in the South Bronx.

1976: Grandmaster Flash and the Furious Five bring in a new era of MCs.

1984: Russell Simmons and Rick Rubin team up to launch Def Jam Records.

2004: P. Diddy launches the "Vote or Die!" campaign. He encourages young voters to participate in the presidential election.

1988: Hip-hop gets its own show on MTV, *Yo! MTV Raps.*

1994: Queen Latifah wins the Best Rap Solo Performance Grammy for "U.N.I.T.Y."

1999: Eminem's *The Slim Shady LP* sells 4 million copies.

1987: Public Enemy stuns audiences with their first record, *Yo! Bum Rush The Show.*

2007: Grandmaster Flash and the Furious Five are inducted into the Rock and Roll Hall of Fame. They are the first hip-hop group to receive this honour.

1992: Dr. Dre releases *The Chronic* and pushes gangsta rap into popularity.

GLOSSARY

authentic real or genuine

bling flashy jewellery sometimes worn to show wealth

borough one of the five divisions of New York City, each of which is also a county

mogul important or powerful person

needle drop action of dropping the needle on a specific spot on the record

phenomenon something very unusual or remarkable

rebellious disobedient to the people in charge

rhythmic having a regular beat in music or dance

sample take a portion of one song and reuse it in another

scratch action of moving a record back and forth while the needle is dropped

tag write one's name in paint or permanent marker on someone else's property

turntable circular, revolving surface used for playing phonograph records

underground artist artist who is not signed to a major record label and is not considered part of the mainstream